My Spiritual Heritage

My Spiritual Heritage

Faithe Hoover Musser

VANTAGE PRESS
New York

FIRST EDITION

Published by Vantage Press, Inc.
516 West 34th Street, New York, New York 10001

Manufactured in the United States of America
ISBN: 0-533-12729-7

Library of Congress Catalog Card No.: 98-90153

0 9 8 7 6 5 4 3 2 1

This is a true story
about Irvin Hoover,
Anna Lady, and Carrie Deemy,
"Papa," "Mama," and "Mother."

1

My Mama was fatally burned on New Year's morning, January 1, 1927. While she was getting breakfast, a small can of kerosene that had been placed on the reservoir of the stove fell on the hot stove, scattering flames over her. Papa was absent from the house at that time and couldn't extinguish the fire. He was at the neighbors' getting cattle that had gotten out during the night. The house was not burned. Mama left five girls, ages ranging from nine years through three months old. I was the middle girl, five years old. My name is Faithe. My two older sisters, Rozella, nine years, and Virgie, seven years, were not at home, as they had stayed at a relative's house during the night. I was the oldest girl at home.

My three-year-old sister, Eunice, and I were at the table eating breakfast. My baby sister, three months old, Mary Lou, was upstairs in the crib asleep. When the accident happened, Mama ran out the kitchen door screaming so loudly that the neighbors one-half mile away heard the screaming and drove up to see what was going on, only to see Mama lying on the yard; rolling and screaming, smothered in flames. I grabbed my three-year-old sister's hand and ran down the lane and road, crying loudly, and wondering why the neighbors didn't pick us up and take us back home, but as I said earlier, they were in a hurry to get where the screaming was.

Finally, Papa arrived home, as he had heard the screaming too. He turned his horse around, got home as fast as he possibly could, and put out the fire. Mama lived five hours. She was a beautiful corpse. The wind blew the flames from her neck downwards. Her face and blonde wavy hair were not touched. A miracle, I'd say. Papa kept saying, "If I only had been there, I would have taken a blanket and smothered out the flames." After he kept saying that, I thought I should have done that. I told no one what I was thinking, but it bothered me a lot, even if I was only five years old. I later knew I was too young to even think of doing that.

Papa was of modest means. As I said earlier, my baby sister. Mary Lou, was only three months old. One couple who was very well off financially offered Papa a large sum of money to let them adopt her. There were a few seconds when he thought that might be well; but then he said, "With God's help, I'm going to keep my five girls together."

Our Mama's folk, our Grandma and Grandpa Lady moved in with us for a few years to help out. We girls loved them very much, and it took a big load off Papa. My folk were very religious and depended on God a lot for help and guidance. On Mama's deathbed, she said to Grandma, "Take care of my babies." The funeral day had come, a very sad one for us. Nearly a thousand persons were present and after the church was filled, a throng stood outside. What a crowd!

The days came and went. Papa would come home tired from working on our farm. He was down and somewhat depressed. Then one day when he saw us girls out playing baseball, something "snapped" in him and he thought, *That's what I have to live for!*

It was now getting into three years and Papa still hadn't remarried. People would ask him, "Why don't you get married?" His answer to them was, "I not only have to look for a wife, but a mother for my five girls." That meant a lot to me later in life, to think we meant that much to him.

I remember so vividly the next day after Mama burned to death. Our parlor was filled with relatives sitting around in a circle. I was wondering why Mama didn't show up. My Aunt Minnie picked me up and held me on her lap. I kept asking for Mama. I knew very well what happened to her because I saw it, but it just seemed strange to me that Mama wasn't around. Then the day of the funeral, when we were at the cemetery, I saw Mama's casket and said, "Don't put Mama in that big hole." It was hard on me emotionally all right as you'll read in the latter part of the book.

Then I recalled the day before Mama had that terrible accident, I was at the end of the large ironing board with my little iron, ironing, while Mama was doing her regular ironing with her big iron. I shall never forget that and talked about it for some time after she was buried. Quite something for a five-year-old to witness, seeing her mama burn to death.

After Mama died, Grandma and Grandpa stayed at our house to help care for us five girls. Papa would always want to take us to a small town named "Industry." Grandma wouldn't always let him take us, as she said we needed to get to bed early. We would have to go to Sunday school the next morning. Papa would listen on her once in a while, but one Saturday night, he told Grandma he was going to take us with him. We girls always loved that. It was fun. Papa would give us each a penny and we would have fun spending it. Then each Saturday night Papa would buy a large sack of candy, and when we got home he would make five piles and count the candy out, making a nice handful of candy for each of us girls. I shall never forget. That was a big highlight in our lives. We five girls would always sit in front in church with Papa. When our little sister would fuss a lot and cry, he would always take Mary Lou outdoors and spank her. When they came back in, she was quiet. Little spankings did us all good. We learned to behave.

We five girls would get up in front of the church Sunday mornings and sing for the congregation. People called us the "Stair step sisters," as that is how we looked, each two years apart. We would also sing "special numbers" at various other places. We each had a talent for music, especially singing and playing the piano. We weren't bashful about it, as we enjoyed doing it. Papa, Grandma, and Grandpa were very proud of us.

People often referred to Papa as "Job" in the Bible, as he had had so much trouble and suffered so much. One time his body was covered with open sores called carbuncles, big sores all over his body, and they were so very painful. They lasted for some time. He went to doctors and finally started to heal. Doctors were puzzled how they ever started. Thank God he was healed.

The first of us five girls, Rozella, got her finger stuck in the corn sheller. The cogs of the sheller were shelling corn off the cobs, and she got her finger in there. Papa saw her and quickly turned the corn sheller off, but he was too late. Her finger was taken off down to the knuckle. She lives with it today and thinks nothing of it, and the only thing that is negative about it is that she can't play the piano too well. It could have been worse. It could have been her whole hand, if Papa hadn't noticed it when he did. Thank God.

One day someone invited Papa up to Iowa to a Church Love Feast. We lived in Kansas. Our church throughout the states always had one yearly. He went and there he met a lady whom he somewhat liked from the first; and after he came back home from Iowa, he started corresponding with her. One day Papa announced to us three older girls that he had found a nice lady whom he wanted to correspond with. He later said, "You always called your mama 'Mama.' " He wanted us to call this one "Mother." This surprised us girls. Our older sister Rozella got us older two girls together and informed us we were not to call her "Mother," as that was a nicer name than "Mama." We agreed. Later, I'll tell you why Papa asked that of us girls.

Papa had so much bad luck in his life. One Sunday when we were in church, which was always the case on Sundays, a neighbor came into our church and told him our chicken house was on fire. By the time Papa arrived home, our chicken house was burned to the ground, with all the chickens gone. This indeed was a great loss, as Papa depended on the egg money to help buy our groceries. But we managed somehow.

Youngsters today have it easy in regard to school closings because of snow or icy roads. We four girls were not so fortunate. I remember one school we went to was a little over one-half mile away. We walked to school in all kinds of weather. It had been snowing and blowing and drifting throughout the night. We had to get up early, go to the barn to milk the cows in zero weather, then wash the separator before going in for breakfast. After the breakfast dishes were done, we got dressed for school. There were high drifts in our lane and down the road. We had bundled up well with our shoes and mittens. I remember when we walked through the snow banks one leg would sink down into the snow bank and I would lift it out and take a step and pull it out while the other leg went into the snow bank. That is how we got to school. We were freezing cold carrying our dinner pails. We were crying when we got to school.

There was a large furnace in the middle of the one-room school house with all eight grades. Our teacher was so kind to us. She lived just across the road from the school house. She had basins of cold water for us to put our hands in to take the "sting" out of them. We would leave them in the water for minutes before they were ready to come out of the water. Our clothing was wet with the snow on us from the time we left our homes. We laid our mittens around the stove to dry before putting them on to go home after school. Then after school was out we put on our heavy coats and mittens to track in the snow again. That's the way it would go nearly all winter. When we got home, we would again take off our coats, mittens, and overshoes and warm up by the coal stove before we had to go out to milk the cows. What a life. Well, we survived. The children today don't know how fortunate they are. I almost "cringe" when I think about those days of snow and ice, but we lived through them and were none the worse for having gone through that.

When we would go to church—and church was never canceled because of weather—we would heat bricks in the oven to keep our feet warm. We would drive to church in a big wagon with a team of horses pulling it. We children thought that was exciting, although we felt nearly frozen when we got to church. Papa, Mama, and we five little girls were in the wagon. I remember one Sunday we drove past our house to go to visit friends of ours for dinner. They had a large family of ten children. Dinner was late as they had to peel the potatoes when they got home from church, as nothing, except the dessert, was fixed before church. After dinner we children would help with the dishes and then when they were finished, we would go outdoors and play in the snow with a small sleigh and someone pulling it. "Those were the good ol' days." Memories are cherished even today.

Then around four o'clock we would leave for home to change our clothes and dress to go out in the snow and were told to milk cows, before going to church in the evening. We would rarely miss school or church in those days. We have it so nice now. Papa and Mama went through a lot to keep us five girls healthy and from getting sick, although we would get diseases such as measles, whooping cough, chicken pox and colds, and get over high temperatures that we would run occasionally. A doctor never was called. We would have to go to see our doctor if we were very sick. We five children today are living and in reasonably good health survivors from those "by-gone" days.

When I was seven years old, we five girls and Papa were driving to evangelistic meetings called "camp meeting," in a large tent. Papa kept telling us to sit down in the back seat and not stand up. I didn't listen very well. I was standing up by the door, and it came open and I fell out of the car. Papa looked in the rearview mirror and saw me lying back there on the road. I was unconscious and all bloody. He took his good suit coat off, wrapped me in it, and rushed me to our family doctor. I finally came to, and wasn't seriously hurt, thank God. After the doctor had me all bandaged up, Papa drove to the small town called "Industry" and bought me a doll. I was feeling better already, but I don't believe I stood up in the back seat again.

Then a real disaster came into our lives. Let me tell you, though, firstly, Papa and this lady from Iowa were going to get married, and they had the wedding day set. A few days before the wedding day, a cyclone—now they call them tornadoes—came one night to our farm. It just happened our baby sister, Mary Lou, was staying at our uncle and aunt's place that night. It was fortunate she did. We four girls were in bed, and the windows were all broken and glass was all over the floor. Of course, we were all barefooted, so Papa took two girls in his arms and carried them downstairs to the cellar, then went up and got the last two. Shortly after he was down the cellar steps, the house moved and closed up the stairs. Had he had to go back up-stairs and get the last girl, Mary Lou, they would not have made it, and no doubt been killed. God works in mysterious ways, his wonders to perform. In the meantime, Grandma and Grandpa had already gotten to the cellar. We girls were so frightened and were screaming as we heard the wind blowing and roaring, with crashing noises outside. Finally, after what seemed hours, but was evidently minutes, it was over. There was a small opening in the cellar where the wind moved the house over leaving space just large enough to crawl up and out of. I remember Papa pushing each of us four girls up out of the cellar, I don't rightly recall how Grandma and Grandpa got out. Papa, I'm sure, crawled up and out. What a mess outside. Mattresses were lying in trees. Clothes and articles were lying all over the farm yard. The dresses that our church "sewing circle" had made for us girls for the wedding were gone. Neighbors reported seeing some of them a mile away. It was fortunate Papa had left his wedding suit in town the day before. The sewing circle hastily made dresses again for us girls.

After we got out of the cellar and saw part of the damage, which was terrible, Papa and we four girls walked a half a mile to a neighbor's house to spend the night. Oh yes, Papa lit a lantern to help us get to our destination. The neighbors were willing and ready to have us and care for us. I wanted to go, yet there were electric lines down all over, and we had to be extremely careful where we walked. Papa walked back to the house to stay the rest of the night; however, when he got back it started blowing and the wind was howling. He was afraid another storm might come, so as his car was in working order and not blown away, he got in it and went a few miles away to stay with his mother, Grandma Hoover. It was very late at night,

8

and she welcomed him with open arms. I'd better say here that Grandma and Grandpa, who stayed with us, got in their car and went to their home only a few miles away. Both cars were in working order. Another "miracle," I'd say.

The next morning came daylight, what a terrible mess. The house was wrecked, part of the roof gone, the barn shed in which we kept the machinery, the wash room and silo were all a wreck. Papa's favorite horse was still standing with a two by four lumber driven through its belly. Papa then went and got his gun and shot it, to get it out of its misery. I didn't mention that the house was all painted and fixed up for Papa's new bride. He wrote her, told her about the cyclone, and that there was nothing nice to bring her home to. She wrote back and said, "A tent or a cottage, why should I care?"

At once, a chicken house was being built and that was where we were going to live until the house could be built. The chicken house was finished, and quickly, with the help of neighbors. We girls had a great time living in that! The wedding day was approaching; and the chicken house was fixed so it could be lived in. Papa and we five girls drove up to Iowa. The wedding was a lovely one. We then drove back to Kansas, to our place of living, several days after the wedding. In the meantime, if you remember, we girls were not to call her "Mother"; in fact, we never called her anything. Evidently this bothered her and evidently she spoke to Papa about it. So Papa got us girls together and confronted us about it. Rozella then told him we weren't going to call her "Mother," as it was a nicer name than Mama. Papa shed tears and understood, and then he mentioned why he requested it. He said we always called our real mama "Mama," and he wanted us to distinguish between the two. He wanted us to keep calling her that, because he wanted us to never forget our Mama, but to talk about her and to know which one we were talking about. We girls readily understood, and from then on, it was "Mother." She was a very good wife and a kind mother to us five girls. Papa did well in waiting for three years to get her.

2

In approximately two years, Mother became pregnant. We were blessed with a baby brother, and Papa had a son at last. I remember before leaving to go to a one-room school house, with all eight grades, I kissed my brother whose name was Herbert. That thrilled me, the idea of saying I kissed a boy, so I went to school and told my classmates, "I kissed a boy this morning." I then explained to them what it was all about. They were happy for me. Oh yes, I remember when the neighbors and church people heard it was a boy, they said, "Here we go—five boys now," knowing that Mama had five girls.

The chicken house was a good place to live when there was no other house, but the new house soon began taking shape. It was a beautiful little bungalow. I mentioned earlier how much bad luck Papa had. Well, he went bankrupt. This was about more than he could take. He was a hard, very hard worker. His cousin from Pennsylvania heard of his plight; and agreed to rent him 160 acres of land nearby to farm. There was a large house, along with other farm buildings. Papa and Mother, along with us girls, were happy for another chance! Papa did well. He bought the farm from his cousin, and when he passed away later, he was debt free. A hard worker he really was. After Herbert was here, another boy, Glenn, was born. So now there were seven of us children. Then after several more years, a girl was born, named Carol. Then there were eight.

Getting back to our one-room school with all eight grades, one day as I was standing up to be dismissed for recess, my cousin Aaronetta Dayhoff was sitting behind me and whispered to me, "Faithe, you have blood on your dress." I was frightened, so we girls went outside to the toilet. They had two outside toilets, one for the boys and one for the girls. I pulled the back of my dress around to the front and saw blood. Aaronetta told me I was having my period. I had never heard of that, as Mother never told me about it. I told my cousin, "I can't go back in the schoolhouse with blood on my dress, " so Aaronetta said, "Faithe, you go home and I'll tell Mr. Ritter, our teacher, you went home because you were sick." True, nevertheless. So I went home and Papa, who was so strict, was driving the tractor in a field by the long lane. When he saw me walking up the lane, he thought I had done something bad at school, so he turned his tractor around and started for the house. I got in the house first and Mother asked me what was the matter. I told her, "I have blood all over my dress and what is it?" She knew immediately. Just then she saw Papa coming in the house, so Mother said, "Don't go in. I'll explain. Faithe had blood all over the back of her dress and she is scared. She has her period." So Papa went outside and left on his tractor. Mother told me I had my period saying, "I didn't tell you, but you'll get it once a month." That's all she told me, nothing else. I wondered why and what I could wear to absorb the blood, but I didn't ask Mother anything.

That evening Aaronetta came over to see me and came to the room where I was. She told me a little bit but didn't tell me anything about what to wear while I had it, so I got old towels and sewed pieces of it inside my panties to absorb it. It didn't look good, but how was I know what to wear? I did that until I can't remember how long. I hadn't been told anything about sex and so forth, and I was twelve years old when it happened. That evening when I went out to the barn to milk the cows, Papa treated me especially nice. I never will forget how nice he was to me. I think he felt sorry for me because I didn't know about having periods. I was really shielded. I wonder to this day why my two sisters never told me, because I'm sure they had their periods and never mentioned anything to me. I was too shy to ask.

Girls today know all about their periods and much more, I'm sure. Everything I learned about sex, I learned from my husband on our wedding night. We had a very good and loving Papa, but he said, "If any of you girls get pregnant before you're married, you'll have to leave home." This scared me a lot, but I didn't know what the word "pregnant" meant. So on one of my dates when I was twelve, a boy kissed me and I went into the house when he left. (By the way, he was a few years older than I was.) Well, I told Mother I was pregnant and what happened. Right away she asked, "Is that all?" I said, "Yes." Then she said, "No, Faithe, you're not pregnant." I was relieved, but she still didn't tell me how I could get pregnant and quite a life I had. So ignorant about sex! Getting back to periods, I never even heard about Kotex or Tampax.

Papa was a wonderful Papa, although he was very strict. I'm recalling now about grade school. Our lunch was carried in a small tin bucket, the kind all children carried. I remember for lunch we hardly had much of anything to eat. We would have had enough, but what we had we didn't like. We had homemade bread with eggs in between the bread. The eggs weren't fried, they were soft, and they were cold by lunchtime. Generally, I didn't eat my sandwich, because I couldn't stand soft, cold egg sandwiches. We also had an apple, and that's about all. I ate my apple.

One family of children at school always had peanut butter sandwiches. It smelled so good and so tempting. Every day they had peanut butter sandwiches, and we had cold soft egg sandwiches. Well, I was soon to take my eighth-grade examination one day, and all students had to bring their noon lunch. I never will forget what Papa did, never will I forget. He went to the grocery store and bought fresh baked bread, lunch meat and cheese, bananas, and oranges and a candy bar for my lunch. That was for the day of my exams. I couldn't wait for lunchtime. It seems to me there was something else in the dinner pail, but that's all I can remember now. Yes, I passed my examinations!

Papa needed a hired hand to help him with the harvest, mainly to drive the tractor while he drove the combine. As I hated high school, Papa let me stay home and help him with the farm work. I remember one year Papa said, "Faithe, I trust you to do a better job driving the tractor for combining. I'll pay you fifty dollars," just what his hired hand wages amounted to. I was so happy that I did it. The other girls didn't care for that, as they had to milk the cows, feed the chickens, and do the jobs around the house. They didn't think that fair. You see, our two brothers were still too small to help on the farm. Another girl arrived, named Delores. Now there were nine children, and last but not least, another boy named Harry. This was a family of ten children. We all had a lot of fun, along with fighting, as is the case, I believe, with all children; but we still had a lot of fun.

My two older sisters were old enough to go to college, so our grandparents paid their way to college for two years. They went to Pennsylvania, to our church college, Messiah College. They stayed in Pennsylvania to work after the closing of school. They each got good jobs as maids in rich people's homes.

Again, I was the oldest one at home. Papa was very

particular. When driving the tractor for combining, he didn't like "skippers." I made very few, but when I did, he motioned for me to keep going. He would jump off the combine, take his pocket knife out, and cut the skipper off, then jump on the combine again. That's how particular he was.

Getting back to before my teen years on the farm, Papa was so very ambitious, sometimes, I feel, too ambitious. One day we had hired men out in the field putting up shocks of wheat and oats. Papa figured they needed water to drink, as it was a very hot day. We had a little black coupe with a rumble seat in it. It had one hundred gallons of gasoline lying on the rumble seat. Papa told me to get in the coupe and take water out to the men. I said, "I don't know how to drive." Papa said, "Get in the car and I'll start it, and when you stop, push down hard on the brakes." He told me where the brakes were. The car had a running board on each side. So Papa stood on the running board, started the car, and jumped off, hollering, "Keep driving." It was one and one-half miles to the fields where the men were working. He didn't tell me to slow down when going around corners, so I just held my foot down on the gas pedal. I went around a corner fast and the gasoline barrel slid off into the ditch. I kept going fast until I got to the field. When I got there, I stopped abruptly. The car stopped dead and the motor went off. I was scared to death.

After I delivered the water to the men, I asked one of them to start the car for me. They said, "Can't you start it?" I told them, "This is the first time I drove." They looked aghast but started the car for me and I took off, going fast and running down the shocks they had already put up. I remember the men hollering after me, "Leave one shock standing." I was scared. I got back home and stopped the car, plowing into a large tree. Mother knew all about this

15

and she came out of the house white as a sheet. She said, "Faithe, slide over. I'm going to teach you how to drive." This she did. I learned the hard way how to drive a car, thanks to my wonderful mother.

Today, I am a terrific driver. When we go on trips sometimes, my husband, David, asks me to drive when he needs a break. So I get behind the wheel and drive. Pretty soon I hear him snoring. I know he's asleep. That's how much he trusts me to drive. I had a very interesting but scary life while growing up.

One morning we got around late with the chores. Eunice was a freshman in high school, and I was a sophomore. We missed the school bus and we had a real long lane to walk to where the bus stopped to pick us up. Well, as we were late, Papa let me drive his good white Pontiac to school. Eunice was with me. We got along fine and made it just in time when the classes started. On the way home while driving, I was behind our school bus. The students looked out the back window and noticed it was us. I was going to be smart and show off by going around the bus, so I did. Only I cut in too close to the bus in going around it and hit the fender of the bus. I pulled over and stopped to see the damage to our car. The fender was dented just a little bit, really not as bad as I thought it would be. I was afraid to go home and tell Papa I had wrecked the car. So on the way home, just a short distance, we went out of the way to a machine shop. We asked one of the men working there if he would fix the fender. He looked shocked and said, "No, not now. That will take some time." He recognized us girls as Irvin Hoover's daughters.

So there was nothing to do but go home and tell Papa, which we dreaded terribly. We got home and saw Papa out at the barn. I drove the car into the garage and went and told Papa I had wrecked his car awful. He said, "Let's go see

16

it." He said, "Is that all? That can be fixed." He didn't even scold me. I made it sound like it was wrecked terribly. I thought that was the way to handle it, making it worse than it was. I was foolish, I know. As Eunice and I rode the bus the next day, the students had a lot of fun with me about wrecking the bus. I was terribly embarrassed. I don't remember about the bus, if it was wrecked, but I'm sure Papa saw to it that it was taken care of. He was a good friend of the bus driver. That was another time it didn't pay to show off or be foolish. I learned my lesson well, as I never did anything like that again. In fact, everyone knew me as being a good driver, as was stated earlier.

When Herbert and Glenn were eight and ten, Papa sent them out to the field with a team of horses and stock cutter, with big blades, to work in cutting off the corn stalks, after the corn was picked. They had an accident and Herbert thought Glenn was dead as he lay still. He ran all the way home for help, even with his "cut-up" foot. Papa went immediately to the accident scene and took both boys to Abilene to the hospital. Glenn became conscious. His head was cut badly and Herbert's foot was badly cut. They were in the hospital for days until they recovered enough to go home. We thanked God their lives were spared.

Just a few "tidbits" about our wonderful Papa. When we would combine wheat, Papa farmed on shares. The landlord's load was always rounded out, "heaped up," and Papa's shares were always leveled off. He always saw the landlord's share was plentiful. This made us children so upset, because Papa didn't keep more for himself, but that's the way he did every harvest time.

One time something came up between Papa and his neighbor, and Papa thought he should go over and make it right. He got there after having driven only one and one-half miles and saw this neighbor and apologized. Then when

17

Papa got back home, his conscience bothered him. He drove back again and told the neighbor he wanted to ask him to forgive him, which the neighbor did. That's my Papa!!

I, Faithe, was quite a girl in my early teens. I liked boys a lot. I had three boys whom I corresponded with at the same time. At the end of each letter, I would write "Your Future Wife, love, Faithe." Papa told me not to put the letters in the wrong envelopes. You see, he had a lot of fun with us children, too.

Papa was a lot of fun as well as very strict. When we children were in the house fighting, we would look out towards the barn to see if Papa was coming. When he would come, our mother said, "You can quit fighting now, he's coming," and that's just what we did. We were loving to one another.

Another time, Papa went outside of the house to look for his boots. He looked and looked and couldn't find them. Just before that, he had scolded me for something. I can't remember what it was, but he thought I had hidden them to get back at him. Well, Papa called me and told me to go get his boots. I told him I never had them. He kept yelling at me to go get them. I was crying and praying,

"Dear God, help me to find Papa's boots." Well, God never let me find them because, you see, I never took them. Just then, along came our dog carrying the boots in his mouth. Was I relieved! Papa, with tears in his eyes, asked me to forgive him, which I did, but it still hurt. That's how conscientious Papa was. I admire that in him today.

One time we had revival meetings at our church, and Papa, Eunice—my sister just younger than I— and I went to church. It was winter and nighttime. We were late, so Papa drove fast. The road was clear, but on the other side of the hill, it was icy. We went over into the ditch and the car turned over and lay on its side. We just had gotten a new white Pontiac and it was wrecked. We three were all sitting in the front seat. When the car had stopped, Papa asked, "Faithe, are you all right?" I said, "Yes, but our new car is wrecked." Then he said, "Eunice, are you all right?" She said, "Yes, but our new car is wrecked." Then Papa said, "The car doesn't matter, just so you're both all right." Then Papa passed out. He wouldn't talk anymore. We thought he was dead. So we girls rolled down the window of the car and somehow managed to crawl out. It took an effort but we got out.

There was a farm house not too far from where our wreck was. We saw lights in the window and knew they were home. We knocked, and a man came to the door. We both were crying but told him we had a wreck and we thought our Papa was dead because he wouldn't talk to us. So the man went with us to the scene of the accident and tried and tried to talk to him, but Papa wouldn't answer. Eunice and I both cried harder. Then Papa finally came around and barely whispered, so the man said, "He's alive. I'll try and get him out." He had us girls run back to his house and ask his wife to call a neighbor to help him, so we did. The neighbor was at the scene about the time when we girls got back. I don't know how they did it, but I remember he was out lying on the cold ground. One of the men rushed him to the nearest hospital, and the other man drove Eunice and me home.

When we got home, I remember Mother coming out on the porch and seeing us two girls and another man. Her face got all white. She was horrified. The man told her not to worry, "He's alive, another neighbor rushed him to the hospital." Then the man left and I don't remember much about the wreck after that, but I do know Papa was all right, thank God, and we got another new car, because he had in- surance.

Papa was a very brave man. He wasn't afraid of heights. Farm people filled their silos in the fall of the year. There would be around ten or twelve men, neighbors, who would go to each farm and help. They would fill their silos with stalks that the ears of corn had been husked from. They called it "fodder." They would feed it to cows in the wintertime. As you know, silos were very, very high, and there were steps on the outside clear to the top. Papa would always be the one who would offer to go clear to the top of the silo to check on the fodder. The other men were afraid to go up the high steps. You couldn't look down or you could get dizzy.

One time the men were talking and someone said, "One of us men should go to the top instead of Irvin," our papa. "He has a large family and what if he would fall?" Well, he never did fall. He always kept his balance and wasn't afraid. Papa seemed small in stature when you looked clear up to where he was from the ground, but he wasn't small, just average size. We children and Mama, and later, Mother, were always glad when he came down from the silo. Just to see him up there. God would have his hand on him, I'm sure. That's another incident I will never forget, how brave he was.

I forgot to mention that when we were in harvest time, combining, Papa wouldn't take off for dinner, so Mother would bring dinner out to the field and we would eat there. I remember we had fried chicken and all that went with it. We ate fast, so as to not lose much time, getting back to combining again. Mother was a very good wife and mother.

I remember coming home from grade school one time, and when I got in the house, Mother was at the sew- ing machine making me a dress. She used feed sacks for the material. We often used feed sacks, as our means were modest. There were a lot of beautiful feed sacks. They were so colorful. The dress she made me was a pretty yellow-flowered print. The dress was beautifully trimmed in black rickrack. I was so proud to wear it to school the next day. I'll never forget her doing that for me.

Mother had a niece in Iowa named Elsie Wise. We became good friends. Papa would put me on the train at Abilene, Kansas, and I would go to Iowa to her home in Dallas Center. I'd stay approximately two weeks. We had a great time together. I shall never forget it. Mother also had a nephew named George Wise, whom I learned to know and like a lot. Later we corresponded, and then I'd go visit Elsie again, and naturally, I'd see George. We were in love with each other at a later time, and he asked me to marry him. I was excited and of course I said yes. One day he took me to the city of Des Moines, to buy me an engagement ring. This was a thrilling time for me. I was excited.

Before that, however, I had dates with David Musser, a boy from Abilene, Kansas. We liked each other but weren't serious. Sometime after that David's folks moved to Upland, California, to make their home. David attended Upland College, a church Bible school of the Brethren in Christ.

Shortly after that, George went to Upland, California, to join the Army Air Corps. Papa sent me on the train to go to California, to work as a maid in rich people's homes. I did this for awhile, but I didn't like it. Then I got a job as a "nurse's aide" in a hospital in Upland. George and I would see some of each other, not much though. After he left for his training in the army, David and I started seeing some of each other, however, not seriously. As the days came and went, in my mind, George seemed farther away. I then was seeing David about once or twice a week. We became serious, and finally I wrote George a letter and broke off our engagement. I returned his engagement ring. To this day I have never heard if he had received it or not. I often wondered. Maybe some day I'll ask him if I get up enough nerve.

When I was twelve years old, I worked as a "hired girl" at a farm family's home. They had plenty of money, and they had four children. The two older children were away at college. I don't want to mention any names, so I'll just call her the lady of the house and him the man of the house. I worked hard as I was used to working hard, having to work hard on my family's farm. I knew I pleased the lady of the house. I had to be doing something every minute of the day. When I was finished with my work, I would patch the six-year-old boy's jeans where there were large holes in the knees.

One day the lady of the house said, "Faithe, you are going to work for my husband this forenoon." I was shocked, as I had been hired to help the lady of the house with housework. Well, I went outside and for hours at a time I would turn a handle that would fan wheat, to get the "chaff" out of it so it would be ready to plant in the fall. My arms got so tired I could hardly hold out, but I did. The husband wouldn't let me have a rest period and kept making me turn the huge handle constantly. I thought the lady of the house would have dinner ready, but no. When I finished "fanning wheat," I went inside and no dinner was cooking. The lady of the house said, "Faithe, it is nearly twelve o'clock and dinner isn't started. Run down to the basement quick and get some potatoes to peel for dinner." I was so tired from fanning wheat, but I did as she said. I peeled the potatoes and got them on the stove cooking, then proceeded to get the rest of the dinner around. I was tired and hurt. I wanted to go home and tell Papa how she was treating me.

After dinner when the dishes were all washed and put away and the kitchen cleaned, I went home to tell Papa I couldn't take the abuse from her. I told Papa exactly what I did and what the lady of the house said to me when I got in the house, about no dinner started and how she ordered me around, "bossy," telling me to quickly start dinner, when it was twelve o'clock and I had worked all morning fanning wheat for the man of the house. Then I cried.

Papa was angry. He got in his car and went to see them. He talked to the lady of the house and I don't know what he said, but I know he said aplenty as I was hired to do house-work. He told her I was quitting and wouldn't be back. I loved Papa so much for "telling her off." Papa didn't like it when we were taken advantage of and weren't treated fairly. I loved Papa more, if that were possible, after he did that for me. Oh yes, I was paid three dollars and twenty-five cents a week. I want to mention too, before that happened, I had to go to the pasture every evening and drive all the cows up into the barn to be milked. I wasn't asked to milk them, however. That was my daily "chore," helping the man of the house, and then going in and starting supper, the evening meal. I was more than relieved after Papa set me free from that family.

I also worked for the brother and sister-in-law of the lady of the house. That was entirely different. They were Laura and Harry Kuntz. Laura was pregnant and soon to go to the hospital. They had a boy of two at home for me to take care of besides the housework. That was a joy. The boy was so good and listened well. Laura told me to take a nap every day after the noon dishes were done and put away. She finally went to the hospital and had a baby girl. When she returned from the hospital with her baby, I was on my own, but Laura kept telling me, "Don't hurry, Faithe. Take your time." She was so sweet. I loved the place. Harry,

23

the husband, always was so cheerful to me and thanked me often for the good job I was doing. I worked there for six weeks, which I enjoyed thoroughly. To this day we each send one another Christmas cards every year. I was told they told people how they liked Faithe Musser to work for them.

There were several other incidents while I was working as a "maid" in homes in Pasadena and Upland, California. At one place I was at in Pasadena, the folks didn't have too much financially speaking. I was treated rudely in that place. They liked to "put on the dog," but with modest means. The lady of the house had me order four pork chops for dinner in the evenings. There were four of them, but she didn't tell me to order one for myself. I fixed the pork chops deliciously. I don't know what she thought I would eat, but all I had was cold cereal for dinner. I didn't care for the lady of the house much. They had two children. I was to look after them also, especially in the evenings when the parents went out. The children were spoiled.

One day when the Rose Bowl game was played in Pasadena, they went out for the football game. The lady of the house told me they were having friends in after the game, so she told me to make a large bowl of eggnog. I had never made it in my life and she never even told me how to make it. I fixed it the best I could. She had lots of alcohol for it. I fixed the yolk of eggs and alcohol to taste. I kept pouring in alcohol, and I had to taste it to see how it was. I had never drunk alcohol in my life, so it was something new to me. I didn't taste it more than I had to.

When they came back from the game, the lady came in the kitchen to see if everything was ready, including finger sandwiches. She told me the eggnog was good after she tasted it. It had been very cold on the day of the Rose Parade. There was much laughing going on in the living room where the punch was being served. I felt they had a little too much of the eggnog. Finally when the guest left, I went into the living room and brought out all the cups to the kitchen. There was barely any eggnog left. I threw the remainder down the sink, because I surely wasn't going to finish it.

I got tired each morning ordering four pieces of pork chops or steak. Everything was four. I called on the telephone to have them delivered, so there was no meat for me to eat. I got hungry preparing the dinner for them each evening. I felt misused, so I told the lady I was going to quit. She didn't say much, but I left and was glad to be out of there.

The next place I went to was owned by a couple of elderly people in Upland, California. What a difference. They really had a lot of material wealth. Their house was huge and very nice. This lady always came out to the kitchen to see if I needed any help in fixing breakfast, lunch, or dinner. I told her everything was fine and thanked her for asking. When the husband had to be away all day on business, this lady would always say, "Faithe, I'll be eating alone today, so set two places at the table for lunch, as I hate eating alone." She wasn't too prissy to have me, a maid, eating in the living room with her. I loved the couple very much, and the man always drove me on my days off to my uncle and aunt's place. He was so kind. I worked there until one of their daughters had a lung removed, at a distance from their home, so they both left to go there and be with the family. She hated to tell me as I was out of a job. Well, I felt badly but understood, and I thanked them for being so nice to me. They told my aunt, "We sure like Faithe." My aunt told me that, and that certainly made me feel good.

25

3

A couple of "tidbits" of interest during my last years at home: I somehow liked to live dangerously. Papa had bought a pony. It was coal black and a beauty. But the original owner warned Papa it was a wild pony and to tell the girls to be careful riding it, or even not to ride it at all. Well, I wanted to ride it, so I did. I was going down the long lane at a rapid speed. The pony "reared up" and threw me off. I told them I hurt all over and it hurt awful to move. They went and brought their car to where I was and drove me home. It was getting dark outside. I cried and suffered, so I was helped into bed. I still was suffering in the wee hours of the morning.

Papa finally called up Dr. Wisby, a chiropractor, and the doctor said, "Bring her in right away." It was in the wee hours of the early morning when the doctor examined me and gave me a good and long treatment. He said I was to come back in two days and have another adjustment. So Papa took me back about six times, and I finally got better, but I still hurt some. I took pain pills. Papa soon got rid of the pony. I, for one, was glad it was gone. Seems I had to learn the hard way, which I did occasionally.

Another sweet thing Mother did for me was in the days when enterprising youngsters would send off for small packets of seeds from a catalog for ten cents a packet. You could order something after all the seeds were sold and the money was sent in. I wanted a guitar so badly, so I ordered some seeds. I don't remember how many packets there were, but surely a good many. Well, I received my seeds and at first I was really going strong until it became a chore. So I was falling behind in sales. One day Mother went shopping in Abilene and took my seeds along, which I didn't know about. She stood on the corner of one of the streets in Abilene and sold them to people she knew, and people she didn't know. She sold them all. She actually did this for me. She had to humble herself to stand there on the corner and ask people if they wanted to buy seeds. When she got home from town, she said, "Faithe, you can send off for your guitar now. Your seeds are all sold."

I was so excited and to think she actually did this for me! I was thrilled and I thanked her and thanked her. She evidently thought it was worth it when she saw how happy I was. To this day I shall never forget her doing such a lovely thing for me. I thought she was the greatest! I received my small guitar and was thrilled. My uncle had a hired man who had a guitar. He heard about mine and taught me how to "pluck it." I was doing great until the hired man left. So I just plucked it and plucked it until one of the strings broke. That was the end of my little guitar, but not the end of being grateful to Mother for selling my seeds.

We had old-fashioned "camp meetings" in the country in a huge tent. We would take our dinner and stay all day. Around noon we would take our lunch out and sit around on the grass and eat. This is where we girls met boys whom we liked a lot, as well as the boys meeting the girls they liked. I remembered I, Faithe, liked to go to camp meetings just to see the boys. We didn't tell Papa or Mother, but somehow I think they knew it all the time. Just another "tidbit" from our childhood days.

Papa was always doing something exciting and nice for us children. One day some of Mother's family was at our place from Iowa visiting. One day Papa took us down to Wichita, Kansas, to pay to ride in an airplane. They did that in those days. Mother stayed home with her sisters from Iowa. I was a little scared, but I got in the plane and rode anyway. I really liked it. It was fun and very exciting. Then, on the way home from Wichita, we stopped and all had ice cream to finish out the day. It was around one hundred miles from our home in the country. Papa always did something sweet, no matter how many troubles he had. I admired him for that.

Things were getting serious with David and me, but I want to put that on hold for the time being. I want to write about my two older sisters. Virgie, the second of us five girls, met a young man in Pennsylvania, and they became engaged. She and Rozella, the oldest of five girls, both quit college and came home then. Virgie and her friend were married and went back to Pennsylvania to stay where her husband, Glenn Hess, lived. They had seven children.

Rozella later became attracted to a young man and they were serious, but later they broke up. Then she learned to know and love a young man also from Pennsylvania. John Thrush was his name. They were married and moved to Pennsylvania to live. They had five children.

Now, I will pick up about Faithe, me, again. While I was working as an aide in the hospital, I had to have an appendicitis operation. This was very sudden. It went well. However, coming out of the anesthesia, I got the hiccups. This lasted quite a while. The doctor was concerned I might injure my incision, but after awhile the hiccups stopped and all was well.

David wrote to my folks in Kansas and informed them of my operation, that it had gone well and I was recuperating in the hospital, a very thoughtful thing for him to do, I thought. My folks appreciated it, too. Then I received a letter from Papa while still in the hospital. It was a lovely and encouraging letter and I cried when I read it. I was homesick after that. He sent several more letters telling me to get well and rest and not go back to work too soon. After a few weeks, I was able to return to my nurse's aide job.

After a while, David and I were seeing each other often. It became serious, and he asked me to marry him. I said yes, so shortly after that, I returned home to get ready for the wedding. You see, David was a junior in college and had one more year to go. We decided on his working part-time, and going to school full-time to finish his senior year. This meant very little income, and he reminded me it would be hard for a while. We were married, nevertheless. For some years we served in the ministry.

Being a pastor and a pastor's wife, especially, was very hard. The whole church watched me, Faithe, to see if I was dressed modestly. In those days "modestly dressed" played a big part in the life of a pastor's wife. Her actions were watched closely. I felt it terribly, and it was hard on me. They watched your children, in our case two sons to see if they behaved and particularly the disciplining of them. As to our salary at one church, which I'll not mention, they didn't have a "set" salary given to us. Once a month the offering plate was passed for the pastor and his family, and I'll never forget the offering for that whole month came to four dollars. We could hardly believe it. It was a great disappointment to us, as we had no other income. So finally the school board of one grade school asked David to teach at their school. He at once said he would. He had to teach, as that was the only means of support we could count on. He also was pastor there for a few more years. I can't recall the church congregation minding his teaching on the side. I really think some people were glad, as they didn't have to support us, which they never did anyway.

That was only one church. Another church where he was pastor, they had a set salary, for us, which we really appreciated. When we think of pastor's salaries today, we can't hardly believe how much they're given, but we don't begrudge them. In our mission work for one year, our salary by the church board was twenty-five dollars for three months. We had to buy car tires, everything, with that salary. We had no insurance given to us, as they do today to pastors. The roads were impassable there at times, so we walked to church. We would walk down a large hill in winter and summer. The roads were muddy during summer months and covered with lots of snow in winter months. We dressed very warmly to walk such a great distance, but that was a hard, but good experience for us. It made us appreciate the salary given us at this one particular church. Such was the life of missionaries and pastors and their families in those days.

David and I went back to California, to the rented apartment that he had secured while he worked and was finishing his senior year. I must confess it was a struggle. Sometime later, after he finished college, the mission board of our church wanted us to go to Knifley, Kentucky, in mission work with a college debt. At that time, I was pregnant, but my doctor advised us to go before the baby arrived. So we went by Pullman on a train, and we had the upper berth to get up into for the night, a very hard thing to do for someone who was pregnant about seven months. But we managed and got to Kentucky with a nurse waiting for us as the train pulled in. I was feeling good. I stood the trip well, although I nearly had a miscarriage during the first few weeks of my pregnancy. I was pushing heavy furniture around while David was in school, and the doctor was called. He put me in bed for a few weeks. David didn't like that I was moving furniture, but knowing me, it couldn't wait. It just had to be done before he got home from school. Ha!

Our son Kenneth David was born on August 2, 1944. He weighed not quite six pounds. He had a lot of black hair, a very pretty baby. The Kentucky people told us we sure didn't need to be ashamed to take him to church as he was so beautiful. He had seven-month colic, and when a few months old he came down with pneumonia. David and I were worn out, and we took turns greasing his chest with "Vicks." Where we lived it was almost impossible to go see a doctor. Well, the Lord and the Vicks did it. He got well. We both were so worn out. Our workers who lived with us in the parsonage thought it would be good if we would go to Kansas for two weeks to visit my folks in Abilene, so that is what we did. Kenneth cried, it seemed, nearly the whole time traveling by bus. Papa met us at the bus depot. Shortly after we got home, we took Kenneth to the doctor, and he said he needed his formula changed. So we did that. However, he continued to have colic. We had a nice visit and rest with my folks, and it was soon time to return to Kentucky. We were there one year, and David was voted in to be the pastor of our church in Kansas near where my folks lived. We were there seven years. David taught school while he was preaching, as our pay was at a minimum, to help make ends meet. He taught in a one-room school with all eight grades. This one morning it was snowing, and he walked one and one-half miles to school, thinking it could possibly drift and he would be unable to get his car home. The snow became heavier and heavier, and then the wind came up.

It developed into a blizzard. Traveling was treacherous. We lived right by the highway where traffic was heavy. One could hardly see across the road, it was snowing and blowing so hard. The school board had called off school, but this

I didn't know, as telephone wires were down and we couldn't communicate. The boys, Ken and Chuck, came home from grade school early so that made me very grateful. I was worried for David, very worried, and didn't know if he had started home and was somewhere in a snowdrift frozen, as it was very, very cold out. The temperature was falling drastically.

There was a knock at the door. Two K P and L men were stranded and asked if they could stay the night. They couldn't see to drive; the blowing snow made it impossible. I was glad to take them in. About fifteen minutes later, another knock at the door. This was a bakery truck driver and he said he saw a light in our window and got that far on foot. He wanted to stay the night. I had one extra bedroom and already three men. I thought we could make out, though. About then, another knock at the door, and there were three college students, two boys and one girl, who were on their way home to spend Thanksgiving. I quickly told them to come in. I had three men, two college boys, and one college girl. I was thankful for the girl. We had neighbors who were close enough we could holler to, and they would hear us, so I went outside and screamed loudly. Sure enough the owner heard me. He came over and I told him of our plight. He offered to take the bakery man and the two college boys. So, I still had two K P and L men, and one college girl. I put the men in the spare room, and the girl slept with me. First, though, I fixed them something to eat.

What I didn't know, though, was that David had to stay at school, as one family of five was still there. Their parents had not been over to get them yet. David ran out of fuel practically and told the students he would break up the chairs and tables to keep them warm if he had to. One lady on the school board said she could not sleep with the teacher and students still in the schoolhouse, so they decided to go in with a wagon and team of horses to take them to board members' homes. They had a lantern to see by. What I didn't know was that our neighbors, who kept three of my men, had two telephone lines. David called them on this one certain line and told the man to come over and let me know he was safe. Then, and only then, could I go to bed and relax a bit. I slept very little, though. The next morning, I gave the people breakfast, and they set out to find their transportation. It was still snowing out, but the wind had gone down considerably, so at least they could see. I supposed everything went well, as they hadn't returned. David soon came home riding a horse loaned him by the farmer with whom he had stayed the night. He left the horse go on his own, to his former owner. The telephone lincs were restored the next day, and we were happy our family was all together again. We were so thankful to see our husband and father safe. The K P and L office had a magazine they put out weekly. Since I kept their men overnight, they came and interviewed me the next day. They listened, thanked me, and then took a picture of the boys and me and our dog. They sent me their magazine and it was all printed in it. I still have it. A night to be remembered forever.

I remember also a time when we lived in the house on the corner of the busy highway. Ken and Chuck were outdoors playing. I was in the house getting supper. My brother Harry was hauling truck loads of wheat into Abilene when he saw the boys and stopped to take them for a drive to Abilene with him. He never gave it a thought except as something to do for the boys. He knew he wouldn't be gone too long, so never told me he was taking them. About that time, I went outside and didn't see them anywhere. I called and called. The close neighbors heard me and I asked if the boys were over there. They said they weren't. I got frantic. I called neighbors all around us and the boys weren't any-place around. Well, living on a busy highway on the corner, I just imagined someone picked them up and ran off with them. I was worried sick. I cried and I prayed. After one half hour or longer, my brother stopped by and let them out. I was outside and crying. I told him never to do that again without telling me. I told him how scared to death I was and thought surely they had been taken and kidnapped. He was so sorry. He told me he had just seen them out playing and thought he would take them for a drive, as it wouldn't be long. He said, "Oh, I'm so sorry, Faithe. I didn't think I'd be gone long, but I promise I'll always tell you when I do some-thing like that again." I forgave him. I was just so happy to see them, and hugged them a lot.

Before going further, by now you know we had another son, Charles Wesley, weighing ten pounds and two ounces. He didn't look like a brother to Kenneth. They were so dif-ferent. There was four years' difference in their age. I had an awful long time of delivery; the baby was so big. I was in the hospital ten days from such a hard delivery. When I went home and got inside the kitchen door, I collapsed. I was so weak and tired. David's mother came from Califor-nia to help me with the baby until I got my strength back. She was a dear.

Finally I was going strong and gaining strength. Chuck, as we called him, was a delightful baby. He lay in his bassi-net cooing and was so playful. We often said he wasn't even any trouble. He hardly ever cried and was a joy. I had wanted a girl, but I told David, "If it is another boy, let us hope they are different." We often thought I got my wish. We loved them both very much, however. Many years have gone by since then.

Now, I want to recall about my sister Eunice. Mother had a breast removed that was malignant, so Eunice put off her marriage for a while to care for Mother and help with the younger children. A very lovely thing for her to do. Mother was recovering for a few months, close to a year. She healed nicely and gained back her strength.

Many years have now come and gone. By this time Eunice, Mary Lou, Herbert, and Glenn have all been married and have children. Several years later Carol married and now has two boys.

Among the most dramatic experiences of my life was the death of Papa. His death meant the end of much suffering and hardship. In addition to the cyclone and the fire, which I have written about, was the death of his older brother and an explosion in their home. Papa's older brother, Harry, was thrashing wheat in the field one day, along with a number of neighbors. When Harry left home that morning, his wife, Sarah, said, "Be sure and come home for dinner today, as I'm making ice cream." Harry said, "Oh, you can be sure I'll be home." Well, he never made it home. He got caught in a pulley belt, which was moving at a fast rate of speed and tore his leg. He was killed instantly. Papa idolized his brother and was in shock for many days to come. Just another tribulation that Papa went through in his young life of sixty-eight years.

The other dramatic experience that Papa and Mother had was in the farm home. Our son Ken had been staying with his grandparents for six weeks, while David, our son Chuck, and I were in Dallas Center, Iowa, holding Bible school for a series of weeks. My brother Harry was still at home, along with my two sisters Carol and Delores. Harry and Ken had gone to the pasture to bring the cows in for an early morning milking. Our son Ken told my brother and his uncle Harry a loud noise they heard sounded as if the heavens opened up. Ken thought the noise they heard was too loud to be thunder. Harry said, "No, Ken, it sounded like a big explosion." They forgot about the cows and made a dash for the farm house. What they encountered upon entering the gate of the farm house proved to be true, an explosion. The furnace in the cellar had indeed exploded. When the furnace exploded, silverware placed on the table for breakfast were sent flying to the ceiling top. Fork marks had been imprinted in the ceiling top. Parts of the kitchen area were in ruins, as were most of the other rooms, including the upstairs. There might have been cuts and bruises to show for it, but other than that, they were all spared. When Ken was walking through the upstairs, he slipped on some ripped apart floor boards as he fell halfway to the basement. He had an ugly scar on his side for many years to show for it. By divine providence, no one was in the dining room at that time, not even Mother. Just another of the many unforgettable experiences of Papa's and Mother's tribulations.

When the doctor told Papa he should get off the farm because of his diabetes and heart, he didn't want to, and he stayed on the farm several months after. He kept saying, "I want to die on the good earth that I farmed all these years." One morning my sister's husband went out to the farm with Papa, as Papa was staying at their place at that particular time. Virgil, my sister Carol's husband, was mowing the grass around the place. Papa took the scythe and cut tall weeds and grass, but he evidently felt something coming on and went into a shed with a dirt floor. That is where Virgil saw him sitting on the ground leaning against the shed. He was dead. Virgil called the coroner and Papa was pronounced dead on the coroner's arrival. He was out of all trials, troubles, and tests, and now he is with the Lord. My brother-in-law Virgil had my husband, David, come to our house to tell me Papa was gone. Virgil knew David should be the one to tell me, as he knew how hard I would take it, which I did. It hit me hard.

Papa had been at our place for supper the evening before he died, and we had sloppy joes in a bun. Papa was kidding around, saying, "Slippery, sloppy joes." He was a great person, even in suffering. He kept saying that night how much he loved his children, and "all the in-laws and out-laws." This was a cute saying he used so much. He was a fun-loving person. Just before our son Kenneth had taken him back to Virgil's place, Papa kept complaining about how his head hurt. There was tremendous pain the way he went on. You could see it in his face. The doctor said a stroke was coming on him then, as he died with a heart attack and stroke combined. He was only sixty-eight years when he died. He sure did a lot of living and suffering. He had many trials and tests in those years when he was here on earth. Mama was thirty-four when she died.

4

When Papa died it was a very sad occasion, but at the same time, we were happy that all troubles and suffering he knew were over. We knew he was with the Lord. Our older son, Ken, loved his grandfather so very much, truly just worshiped him. On the day of the funeral, we were in the church basement eating lunch before the funeral service. When Papa died, we all cried, except Ken. I couldn't understand why Ken never cried as he idolized him. When we were eating lunch, Ken came up to me and said, "Mother, I feel terrible sick." I went and got Dr. Dale Eshelman, our sister Mary Lou's husband. I told him Ken never cried at all and said, "He's terrible sick." Dr. Eshelman said, "Send him to the little room upstairs and I'll go get my bag out of the car." Dr. Dale gave him, Ken, a shot and in minutes Ken was crying and crying for some time. Dale gave him a shot, which brought the crying on. After he had his cry, Ken said, "Mother, I feel so much better," and he looked so much better. Dale sure knew what to give him. An incident I'll never forget. After the funeral and especially during the funeral, Ken even cried some. Ken was affected so terribly by his grandfather's death, that he was all tight inside and couldn't let his feelings out, until the shot. So good we had a doctor there that day. To this day, Ken talks about Papa, his grandfather, with great feelings for him and all he was to him.

During this time, David was working for J.C. Penney's

as a salesman for a few years. Then he got started selling Kirby sweepers. It was slow going for a while, but once he got started well, he became the top salesman, many a time. He worked for Kirby about ten years until he was transferred to Little Rock, Arkansas. Oh yes, he resigned from the ministry at Abilene, Kansas. I hated somewhat to move from our cozy home, but it was a promotion, so he accepted it.

The movers made an appointment to come and load up all our furniture to take to Little Rock. This they did. Our son Kenneth was back in Pennsylvania attending our church college, "Messiah College," at this time.

David drove me and Chuck down to Little Rock in my new red Valiant, a bonus from Kirby. He put us up in a motel while he flew back to Abilene to care for his business there, which he would be leaving, and then drove his car back down to Little Rock. I saw a realtor while he was gone and looked at various houses, to buy the one I liked. When David got there, I already had bought a lovely house. He was surprised and happy. After the deal was completed, we went to live in our new house.

I was not feeling good at all and didn't know why. The truckers brought our furniture several days later and unloaded it. The large boxes of small things, such as kitchen utensils, clothing, and odds and ends, they left in the carport. Chuck was a dear, and he helped open the boxes. All of a sudden, my legs started trembling and I could hardly stand up. When I mentioned it to Chuck, he said, "Here, Mother, you sit down on one of the boxes and tell me where the things are to be placed. I'll do the unpacking."

I started getting worse. My nerves were shot and I cried a lot. Chuck kept driving me to different doctors. David was working hard selling Kirbys. No doctor seemed to help me. I started getting worse.

39

We attended church on Sunday, as we were prone to do. We liked the minister a lot, and the people were so friendly. On Thanksgiving Day the pastor and his wife invited us to their home for Thanksgiving dinner. We enjoyed that, but we couldn't stay long because of the way I was feeling. After that the pastor came over to our home and counseled with me. I still grew worse and thought about our brother-in-law in Pennsylvania, who was a medical doctor. So I called Dr. Glenn Hoffman, my husband's sister's husband, and talked to him. He asked me to explain just how I felt. He said, "Faithe, you had a nervous breakdown." Then he told me of a very good hospital in Pennsylvania where they treated people like me.

So, after only being in Arkansas seven months approximately, we moved to Pennsylvania. We left Chuck in Little Rock to attend school, David drove me back to Pennsylvania in my little red car and got me a good motel to stay in, while he flew back to Little Rock, cleared the business up and then drove Chuck and his car to where I was staying. I was glad to see them. Our son, Kenneth, who was in college, came and visited me, when I was alone in the motel. Before David and Chuck arrived, Dr. Hoffman had a minister to come and visit me. He was such a nice person. He counseled with me and had prayer with me. I don't know how long this went on, but it was until David and Chuck arrived from Little Rock.

By the way, by the time this all happened Delores and Harry had been married for some time; all ten children were now married.

David had to set out immediately after he arrived in Pennsylvania to find a rented house to live in until we could find a place to buy. He rented a place in a little town, but it was on a busy highway. I couldn't stand the noise; it made me worse, so he found a quiet little place that we rented.

40

The house was not much, but it was quiet. I gradually grew worse, so I made an appointment at the hospital that Dr. Hoffman told us about. We went and had a consultation with a doctor at "Phil Haven" hospital. I was admitted, but after a few days the hospital staff saw that my doctor was hostile, and so they assigned me to a Dr. Walmer. Immediately I liked him, and he was so nice.

One day he called me into his office and informed me that he was going to have to give me a "shock treatment." I was frightened, but Doctor Walmer informed me it would not hurt me, but that I needed it as I was not getting any better. After the second treatment, I started getting better and better. I was allowed to go home with my husband, David, for a weekend pass. I was to return to the hospital by seven o'clock Sunday evening. I ended up having six shock treatments. I was getting well. I felt so good. The nurses asked me to go with them on their rounds to give out medication to the other patients. I would give them water to drink with their medication. This made me feel real good. I helped them to do this often.

One day a nurse told me I was so good they were going to put me upstairs in a "lovely" room and I could be there alone until I was able to go home for good. The room was lovely, and I felt and knew I was ready to go home for good. I was released from the hospital, after having been there six weeks. I made a lot of friends there, good friends. It was hard telling them good-bye.

After I got home, a realtor took David and me around to numerous houses to look at a house to buy. One house I liked right away, and after consideration we decided to buy it. We are living there to this day. I had to return to the hospital for the doctor to see how I was doing. He was very pleased with my progress, and he always gave me compliments on how lovely I looked and commented how well I was dressed. This pleased me, and David too, because he was always in the room with my doctor and me. I came home feeling good and really enjoyed life again. I was so excited with our new house and had a lot of fun fixing it up.

I asked my doctor one day, "Do you think my having to see my mama burn to death and being the oldest girl at home caused my nervous breakdown?" He said, "Absolutely, without a doubt." I was relieved after that to know why it happened.

Now, I'll let this rest and take you back again.

Papa had had diabetes for years before he passed away, but he got along fine, with Mother giving him "shots" daily. You would never know he had it. He kept working and no one would know he had diabetes just to see him.

One day, Mother was on vacation with Papa and my brother Herbert and his wife, Gladys. Mother recalled having felt something inside of her "pop." After that she became sick, and grew worse and worse, until she went to the hospital and she was told she had a large tumor inside her, which burst. She was full of cancer. We went to the hospital to see her and she looked so bad. She was so sick. I remember having asked her if I could do something for her, and she said, "Yes. The nurses don't have time to comb my hair. Would you do it?" I was pleased to do it. Her hair was so long, she could sit on it. I combed and braided her hair. She said, "That feels so good." The next morning, after we had just finished eating breakfast, the telephone rang and it was word that Mother had passed away. I felt good to think that I had combed and braided her hair just the day before.

Papa took this last blow very hard. Now there were two wives whom Papa had lost in tragedy. The doctor was also treating Papa for heart trouble. He still was on the farm, but had sold all his livestock, so he had freedom and could come and go as he pleased. The doctor told him to leave the farm, but it held special memories and he chose to stay there for awhile. Later he stayed with my sister Carol and her husband, Virgil.

Herbert's wife, Gladys, died with cancer, and Virgie's husband died of a heart attack, but we ten children are still living, though three spouses have died. We ten children are very close. We don't think of half-brothers and sisters. We're just one big happy family. God has blessed us greatly! Herbert later remarried a lovely girl from Iowa. He and his first wife had three children. Later, he and Dawn, his new wife, had a baby girl, Karen. She is in college now. Time sure flies.

We have a family letter of all ten brothers and sisters going around, which comes to each one about every three months. We write in a letter concerning our own family and send pictures occasionally. This keeps us closer together. We started this letter after Papa died, a couple years or so after Mother passed away. He had grown very sick, and it was a blessing he could go. He had many trials and tests in the sixty-eight years that he lived, but he died victoriously. We children were very sad, but comforted because we knew he was with the Lord. That sustained us greatly. Life must go on.

Now about my husband, I remember our bishop's wife told me she did not fall in love with her husband until after they were married. I thought that was strange, but now I know that can be for real, because I fell deeply in love with my husband, David, a while after we were married. It really happened! I know now what love really is. It is a wonderful feeling! Even now, I still love him more, and I am sure it will continue to be so. I wanted to put this in earlier, but I thought I would save the best until later on. We've now been married over fifty-five years.

After we began living in Pennsylvania, David still sold

43

Kirbys for ten years or so, then he became acquainted with a man who sold insurance. He asked David to give it a try, so being master over many things, he got into the insurance business. He got started on the right track. So he went into full-time insurance work, and quit selling Kirbys. He won many trips for us, he did so well. He is still selling some insurance—about one-fourth of his time, being semi-retired. He just cannot quit for good, knowing him. He has extremely nice, congenial people to work with.

Now, I think it is time to talk a little about me. I enjoy playing the piano by ear. I have done that from the time I was around seven years old, if not sooner. I would turn on the radio and hear tunes and quickly turn it off, go to the piano, and play the same tune by ear. I can play nearly everything I hear. I play special musical numbers at our church occasionally. I love doing it. I sit down to the piano and play continuously without stopping as tunes come to my mind, even when I am playing. Then I keep switching to another song, and so it goes. I have a number of tapes filled with piano numbers. At one time I would write poetry, sit down at the piano, and compose the tunes for it. I haven't done that for some time. I may pick it up again. I have a lot down on paper that I haven't put music to. That is a challenge I will probably want to pick it up again.

After my nervous breakdown, I was healed, praise God. I entertained a lot in our home. I loved baking pies and fixing meals. I took pride in that. When we were still in Abilene, and our folks were living, we would get together, and it was "Faithe, you make the pies." That made me feel good. I loved doing it.

We love to take our pastor and his wife, as well as other people out to early breakfast. We also love to entertain in our L-shaped, modest, but nice, home for dessert and coffee. I also enjoy making up new recipes. I try them on David and he loves them.

Now back to my family of ten children. About twelve years ago, we children decided to have a reunion of three days, every three years. Our children, grandchildren, and great-grandchildren come. We are miles apart. The last reunion was this past August 11, 12, and 13. There were forty-some people there. What a wonderful time we had. We cherish our Christian heritage that our family passed down to us. We often talk about Papa, Mama, and Mother. Sometimes we shed a few tears, realizing how rich we are, not money-wise, but in our "bringing up days." We are so thankful for our loved ones who passed on years ago. We are scattered from the East to the West Coast, and in between: California, Colorado, Kansas, Missouri, Virginia, Ohio, and Pennsylvania. Our next reunion will be in 1998, here in Pennsylvania. We have our reunions in various states in which we live. We ten brothers and sisters range in age from fifty-seven years to seventy-eight years.

You might like to know how many children, grandchildren, and great-grandchildren we ten children have—God has blessed us.

Rozella—six children, ten grandchildren, six great-grandchildren

Virgie—seven children, twelve grandchildren, seven great-grandchildren

Faithe—two children, five grandchildren, three great-grandchildren

Eunice—four children, fourteen grandchildren

Mary Lou—three children, seven grandchildren

Herbert—four children, four grandchildren

Glenn—six children, twelve grandchildren

Carol—two children, eight grandchildren

Delores—four children, three grandchildren
Harry—three children, five grandchildren

To date, Irvin, Anna, and Carrie's offspring total one hundred and forty-seven souls.

The best way to summarize this story is by a poem my husband, David, wrote. It tells something about each one of us children while still in our parents' home, something you can read between the lines to really know us.

My Tribute

Irvin and *Anna* were a perfect pair;
their love for each none could compare.
They planned their home with God above
whose presence surrounded them as a Heavenly Dove.

Rozella was the first of ten
as the family's growth soon began.
But early was the burden that she bore,
becoming a mother to her sisters four.

Little *Virgie,* the angel dear,
brought to the family sun and cheer.
And when their tasks her sisters shirked,
gentle *Virgie,* she volunteered to do their work.

Faithe, the middle jewel of the crown,
early learned to find her way around.
Because of love for God's good land,
Ere long she became her father's favorite hired hand.

When *Eunice* did her presence make,
the watching world knew it was no mistake.
Willingly, her wedding plans she set aside,
so with the sick she could abide.

Then arrived *Mary Lou,* number five;
she kept the Hoover family much alive.
And when their spirits were sometimes down,
her melodious yodeling did their farm surround.

And so the perfect circle of seven,
it was on earth a taste of heaven.
But tragedy struck the nest of love;
Mama *Anna* was called to her home above.

Then a virtuous farm maiden *Irvin* sought
and lo, behold, what *God* hath wrought.
Carrie's love, which did much abound,
did the motherless girls her arms surround.

Once again the family grew;
a boy named *Herbert* joined the crew.
Conscientious, for forgiveness did he ask;
to him it was a joyful task.

Then in turn did Glenn appear
for one and all a playmate dear.
His happy, joyful, optimistic view
saved the family from many a stew.

Next appeared sister *Carol,* whose love abounds
with more than enough to make the rounds,
always lending a helping hand
enabling the poor struggler to make a stand.

47

Delores with a heart of gold
was the ninth little lamb within the fold.
Neat and particular, she her Maker planned,
that his wonders and grace she would expand.

Harry then the last of ten,
quickly hastened his work to attend,
serving as a beacon bright,
to guide those lost souls in sin's dark night.

By word and deed the holy loving parents three
for an abundant life to their offspring early on they passed
    the key.
Obey the *Lord* the best you can;
do deeds of love and kindness to each and every fellow
    man.

So as death to each draws near
with *God* our Father there is nothing for us to fear.
May we *All* then hear His words, "My child, well done!"
As one by one life's race is run.

               —David
               1995

Postscript

I am very sorry to report that two of the ten children died two years since the manuscript was written. Rozella, the oldest of the ten children, died on February 1, 1997, and Glenn, the seventh child, died on January 23, 1997. They each died of a massive heart attack. They died within nine days of each other. This was so very sudden to us children and all family members. Sorry the book had to end this way. We feel the loss deeply yet.

Another sad incident occurred on December 2, 1997. Our brother, Harry, sixty years old, died of a heart attack. His wife, Carolyn, and family and we sisters and brothers are all saddened by it. That makes two brothers and one sister who died in the year of '97. All ten of us children had lived for years. Now there is one brother and six sisters who now are living, bringing the number to seven in the original Hoover family.